On-your-own

# Bible Study

# Guide

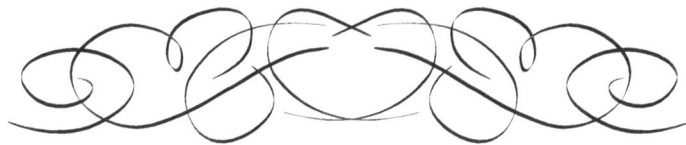

# Book of Jude

# On-your-own Bible Study Guide:  Book of Jude

Text copyright © 2018 Truth in Word Publishing, LLC

ISBN-13:  978-0-9963656-3-5

ISBN-10:  0-9963656-3-X

Truth in Word Publishing, LLC

Bonners Ferry, ID

Website:  www.truthinwordpublishing.com

Email:  editors@truthinwordpublishing.com

**These workbooks can be used both individually and as a group study.**  If you wish to purchase them for a larger group, you may email us at the address listed above.  We will do our best to assist you.

For all high quantity orders, you may contact us through the website or email for discounts.

# Dedicated to . . .

Our children.

And to all who desire to know God more.

"Sanctify them through Thy truth: Thy word is truth."   John 17:17

Truth in Word Publishing     3

# Before you begin . . .

We pray God blesses your study of His Word.  These books are meant to be a help to those who wish to dig deeper into the Bible - and hopefully offer ways and ideas to find the gems of truth that are hidden within it.

We know that in-depth study isn't easy.  That's why we have a burden on our hearts to put these study guides out there for you.  We don't want someone to walk away from the Word because they didn't have the resources to really and truly understand it.

Yet even though we have put together these guides, please remember it is the work of the Holy Spirit to guide you in the way of truth.  We are only fellow believers here to encourage you.

"But the Comforter, which is the Holy Ghost, whom the Father will send in My name, he shall teach you all things, and bring all things to your remembrance, whatsoever I have said unto you."  John 14:26

It is best to pray before we begin studying the Bible; confessing our sins, asking forgiveness, and also entreating God to speak to us through His Word.  If we do this sincerely, He will answer.

And finally, remember this:  how much you get out of studying God's Word is directly related to how much you put into it.  But with a sincere desire to know the truth, He will then lead you in the way everlasting!

In Him,

Lowell and Kendra Graber

# Resources

You will need several resources in order to complete this study guide.  We have listed these below.  Two of these are free programs to download; but if you don't wish to use these, then you will need to purchase a good commentary and concordance.

- **E-Sword Study Program**

  This is a free computer program that has all the resources you could need - only it is digital, not print.  You can download commentaries, Bible versions, concordances, dictionaries, maps, and graphics.  It also lets you search for any word and pops it up wherever it is used in the Bible!  This can go onto a laptop or desktop.  To download, go to http://www.e-sword.net/.  To watch our tutorial on how to use eSword, you can go to http://truthinwordpublishing.com/index.php/videos/.

- **MySword app**

  Like eSword, this is a free program to help you with studying the Bible.  However this is an app for your smartphone and is very handy for quick referencing!  It contains many of the same items as in eSword - commentaries, Bible versions, dictionaries, concordance, and an excellent search function!  You can look for it in the playstore on your phone.

- **Strong's Exhaustive Concordance of the Bible**

  This has all the words of the Bible defined - both the Hebrew for the Old Testament, and the Greek for the New Testament.  You can download this in e-Sword or buy in print on Amazon or in a Christian bookstore.  If there is one resource we would recommend above all others - besides the Bible itself - it would be this one!

- **Commentaries**

  We like to use commentaries by Matthew Henry, John Wesley, and David Guzik - among others.  These can all be downloaded onto e-Sword as well, or you can buy some of them in print.

- **Other good resources**

  We like to use some other resources at times, although they are not needed to complete this study guide.  However, they can be helpful when researching.  Three of these resources are:

  1) *Nave's Topical Bible*

  2) *Rose Then and Now Bible Atlas with Biblical Culture and Background*

  3) *Vine's Complete Expository Dictionary of Old and New Testament Words*

---

<u>Exegesis:</u> *critical explanation or interpretation of a text, especially of Scripture.*

To study Scripture well, believers must take the Scripture within the context it was written. They realize word meanings change over time; therefore, they research what words meant in the language they were written and also how they have changed today. It is imperative to also cross-examine Scripture with other Scripture. The Bible will never contradict itself. The believers research history, culture, meanings, etc. Then they take it all and apply it to their hearts and lives in a practical way.

---

# For the Teacher . . .

If you are using this as a group study guide, there are several things that can make this helpful to the whole class. We have not included a teacher guide since this guide itself is pretty straightforward. However, we will give you some ideas on how to make this meaningful and fulfilling.

**Idea #1:** It is wise to always begin with prayer and a personal examination of our hearts.

*"If I regard iniquity in my heart, the Lord will not hear me."* Psalm 66:18

Sin will hinder the hearing of truth. Therefore, we need to take an honest look at our hearts to see if there is hidden sin, then confess this sin and repent of it. As the teacher, you can encourage this to be done individually while you pray publicly, or if you feel a time of sharing is appropriate. Confession of our faults one to another is also biblical, but it might be best to not require this of your class. This will come when they feel comfortable. Our faith is a personal one and God hears a broken and contrite heart whether it is admitted silently or openly.

Ask the Holy Spirit to guide you and your class in the way of truth. We need the Spirit to help us understand the Word and also to keep our eyes, ears, and hearts open to the receiving of it.

**Idea #2:** This guide is laid out in separate activities and sections. If time is a factor, you can divide up the sections amongst your class. For example: one person can look up the definitions of words in the concordance, while another person tackles the commentary about the hard questions, and yet another can be cross-examining Scripture with other Scripture.

**Idea #3:** Each section is based on roughly 3-4 verses. When you are doing in-depth study, it is difficult to do more than that at a time. We have included a notes page at the end of every study section. You can use this for whatever purpose you wish. Some ideas might be: a place for the class to write down what they have personally learned in the verses, or if you ran out of room while studying the commentary you could write it there. Yet another use could be to write down unanswered questions you have for a well-grounded believer in your life.

And ye shall seek Me,
and find Me,
when ye shall search for Me
with all your heart.

Jeremiah 29:13

He has promised.
In the searching, He will be found.
If we do it with all our hearts.

So let us begin . . .

# Jude vs. 1-3

---

¹ Jude, the servant of Jesus Christ, and the brother of James, to them that are sanctified by God the Father, and preserved in Jesus Christ, and called:

² Mercy unto you, and peace, and love, be multiplied.

³ Beloved, when I gave all diligence to write unto you of the common salvation, it was needful for me to write unto you, and exhort you that ye should earnestly contend for the faith which was once delivered unto the saints.  KJV

---

The book of Jude was written in approximately A.D. 65 - only thirty-five years after Pentecost.  Jude was the brother of Jesus and James and he most likely did not fully believe Jesus was the Messiah until after His death and resurrection.

## DEFINE IT

Look up the Greek definitions of these words in the Strong's concordance.

Sanctified: _____

Preserved: _____

Common: _____

Exhort: _____

Contend: _____

My heart

As you study, ask the Father to reveal Himself to you in these words you read.  If you pray this in sincerity, He will answer.

"Sanctify them through Thy truth: Thy word is truth."   John 17:17

Jude 1:1-3

*Lord, I want to understand*

# UNDERSTAND IT

Search the commentaries for an explanation of these phrases found in your verses.  Then write down the explanations to help you better comprehend it.

"sanctified by God the Father": _____

_____

_____

"when I gave all diligence": _____

_____

_____

"the common salvation": _____

_____

_____

"earnestly contend for the faith": _____

_____

_____

# COMPARE IT

Look up these cross references.  They may help you understand your verses in Jude.

Matthew 13:55          Romans 1:1          Romans 1:6,7          James 1:1

I Timothy 6:12          Titus 1:4          2 Peter 3:1,2

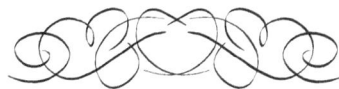

*Earnestly in the New Testament implies that you do it with great intent and purpose.
If we are fighting for this faith, are we doing it half-heartedly . . . or intently and with passionate zeal?*

# COMPREHEND IT    Look the answers up in commentaries if you need.

## What does it mean to be preserved in Jesus Christ?

_____

_____

_____

_____

## How can we earnestly contend for the faith?

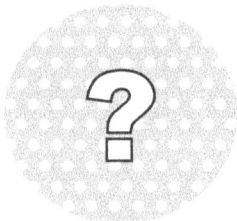

_____

_____

_____

_____

## What are some lessons God has shown you in these verses and how can you apply them to your life?

_____

_____

_____

_____

# Notes

_____

_____

_____

_____

_____

_____

_____

_____

_____

_____

_____

_____

_____

_____

_____

_____

_____

_____

_____

_____

_____

_____

_____

_____

_____

_____

_____

# Jude vs. 4-7

4 For there are certain men crept in unawares, who were before of old ordained to this condemnation, ungodly men, turning the grace of our God into lasciviousness, and denying the only Lord God, and our Lord Jesus Christ.

5 I will therefore put you in remembrance, though ye once knew this, how that the Lord, having saved the people out of the land of Egypt, afterward destroyed them that believed not.

6 And the angels which kept not their first estate, but left their own habitation, he hath reserved in everlasting chains under darkness unto the judgment of the great day.

7 Even as Sodom and Gomorrha, and the cities about them in like manner, giving themselves over to fornication, and going after strange flesh, are set forth for an example, suffering the vengeance of eternal fire.   KJV

## DEFINE IT

Look up the Greek definitions of these words in the Strong's concordance.

Certain men: _____

Lasciviousness: _____

Denying: _____

First estate: _____

Fornication: _____

Psalm 66:18 "If I regard iniquity in my heart, the Lord will not hear me."

My heart

It is necessary for us to confront the unforgiveness and unrepentance that may be in our hearts.

"Sanctify them through Thy truth: Thy word is truth."   John 17:17

Jude 1:4-7

*Lord, I want*

*to understand*

# UNDERSTAND IT

Search the commentaries for an explanation of these phrases found in your verses.  Then write down the explanations to help you better comprehend it.

"who were before of old ordained to this condemnation": _____

_____

_____

"denying the only Lord God": _____

_____

_____

"left their own habitation": _____

_____

_____

"going after strange flesh": _____

_____

_____

# COMPARE IT

Look up these cross references.  They may help you understand your verses in Jude.

| | | | |
|---|---|---|---|
| Galatians 2:4 | 2 Peter 2:1-2 | I John 2:21 | Exodus 14:21-31 |
| Numbers 14:29-37 | Deut. 2:15 | I Cor. 10:5-10 | 2 Peter 2:4-10 |

These ungodly men creep in - meaning they settle in alongside of the true Christians. They become one of us - yet with enough time, their true character is revealed.

"Sanctify them through Thy truth: Thy word is truth."   John 17:17

Jude 1:4-7

COMPREHEND IT   Look the answers up in commentaries if you need.

What are two character traits of the ungodly men (vs. 4) that help us identify them?

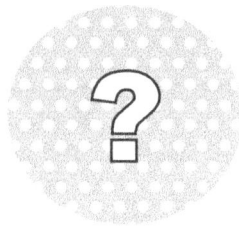

_____
_____
_____
_____
_____

What are three examples of rebellion given in vs. 5-7?

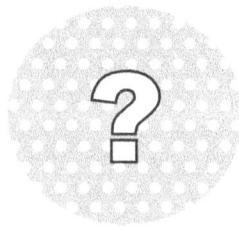

_____
_____
_____
_____
_____

How did God speak to you in these verses?

_____
_____
_____
_____
_____

# Notes

# Jude vs. 8-10

⁸ Likewise also these filthy dreamers defile the flesh, despise dominion, and speak evil of dignities.

⁹ Yet Michael the archangel, when contending with the devil he disputed about the body of Moses, durst not bring against him a railing accusation, but said, The Lord rebuke thee.

¹⁰ But these speak evil of those things which they know not: but what they know naturally, as brute beasts, in those things they corrupt themselves. KJV

Jude was dealing with false teachings that were entering the church. One of these false teachings was that of gnosticism. Among its beliefs, gnosticism promoted the idea of "secret or elevated knowledge". This knowledge was supposedly procured through mystical experiences. But the Bible says we must become as little children to enter the kingdom of heaven. The Gospel is simple and given to all mankind - it wasn't made of elevated or secret knowledge and given to only a select few.

## DEFINE IT

Look up the Greek definitions of these words in the Strong's concordance.

Filthy: _____

Dignities: _____

Archangel: _____

Railing: _____

Corrupt: _____

## MAP IT

Find a map of Palestine (Israel) in either your Bible or eSword. Once you have found it, look for the town of Nazareth where Jude would have most likely spent his childhood years with Jesus. Now find the town of Jerusalem, where Jude would have been eyewitness to the events surrounding Jesus' death and resurrection. How many miles is it between the two cities? _____

"Sanctify them through Thy truth: Thy word is truth."   John 17:17

Jude 1:8-10

*Lord, I want*

*to understand*

# UNDERSTAND IT

Search the commentaries for an explanation of these phrases found in your verses.  Then write down the explanations to help you better comprehend it.

"defile the flesh": _____
_____
_____

"speak evil of dignities": _____
_____
_____

"contending with the devil": _____
_____
_____

"a railing accusation": _____
_____
_____

# COMPARE IT

Look up these cross references.  They may help you understand your verses in Jude.

2 Peter 2:10, 11          Daniel 10:13, 21          Revelation 12:7

Zechariah 3:2             Daniel 12:1

Beware of the people who think they have elevated knowledge . . . and who make fun of what they do not know.  God has revealed Himself to us through His Word and His Son.  We do not need secret knowledge to understand the Gospel - it is there in plain sight for all to see.  Even the simple can understand and believe.

"Sanctify them through Thy truth: Thy word is truth."   John 17:17

Jude 1:8-10

## COMPREHEND IT   Look the answers up in commentaries if you need.

Where else in the Bible is Michael mentioned?  *Tip:  do a word search in eSword or your concordance.

_____

_____

_____

_____

Who holds authority to accuse the devil?  See your cross reference verses.

_____

_____

_____

_____

What does "despise dominion" mean and how can we avoid it?

_____

_____

_____

_____

# Notes

# Topical Search   "spiritual warfare"

Jude speaks of contending for the faith.  This is part of spiritual warfare that believers will be fighting while on this earth.  Using your resources, look up <u>spiritual warfare</u> and see what the Bible says about it. Great resources for this include the search feature in eSword and MySword, the concordance, dictionaries or topical Bibles.  You will have to think of words that pertain to spiritual warfare in order to look it up - the words "spiritual warfare" do not occur in the Bible, but the concept is there in more specific terms.

A few questions that you could answer:

1) What is the definition of spiritual warfare?

2) What are some references I can look up?

3) Who were great Biblical giants that fought this spiritual fight well?  And what was it that helped them in the fighting?

4) Where does a spiritual warrior get his strength and courage?

5) How can I personalize what I have learned and apply it to my life?

_____

_____

_____

_____

_____

_____

_____

_____

_____

_____

_____

_____

_____

_____

_____

# Topical Search

## "spiritual warfare"

_____
_____
_____
_____
_____
_____
_____
_____
_____
_____
_____
_____
_____
_____
_____
_____
_____
_____
_____
_____
_____
_____
_____
_____
_____
_____
_____
_____
_____

# Jude vs. 11-13

11 Woe unto them! for they have gone in the way of Cain, and ran greedily after the error of Balaam for reward, and perished in the gainsaying of Core.

12 These are spots in your feasts of charity, when they feast with you, feeding themselves without fear: clouds they are without water, carried about of winds; trees whose fruit withereth, without fruit, twice dead, plucked up by the roots;

13 Raging waves of the sea, foaming out their own shame; wandering stars, to whom is reserved the blackness of darkness for ever. KJV

## DEFINE IT

Look up the Greek definitions of these words in the Strong's concordance.

Gainsaying: _____

Spots: _____

Clouds: _____

Carried: _____

Fruit: _____

Wandering: _____

"Blessed are the pure in heart, for they shall see God." Matthew 5:8

My heart

There is only one who can purify our hearts. In order to see God, we must have a pure heart in all things. Take your heart to God and ask Him to make it pure, even if it means you must repent of what lies within it.

"Sanctify them through Thy truth: Thy word is truth."   John 17:17

Jude 1:11-13

*Lord, I want*

*to understand*

# UNDERSTAND IT

Search the commentaries for an explanation of these phrases found in your verses.  Then write down the explanations to help you better comprehend it.

"spots in your feasts of charity": _____

_____

_____

"gainsaying of Core": _____

_____

_____

"clouds they are without water":_____

_____

_____

"wandering stars": _____

_____

_____

# COMPARE IT

Look up these cross references.  They may help you understand your verses in Jude.

| | | | |
|---|---|---|---|
| Genesis 4:3-8 | Numbers 16:1-35 | Numbers 22:7 | Isaiah 57:20 |
| I John 3:12 | Revelation 2:14 | Ezekiel 34:8 | I Cor. 11:20-22 |

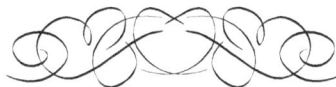

The feasts of charity refers to the time set apart by believers to commemorate the death and resurrection of Jesus Christ - communion.  These feasts of charity were not to be taken lightly, but with each person searching their hearts and repenting of sin . . . realizing what the bread and wine exemplified in their own hearts and lives.

"Sanctify them through Thy truth: Thy word is truth."   John 17:17

Jude 1:11-13

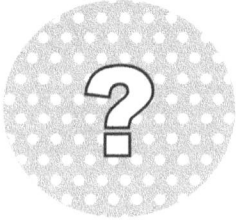

## COMPREHEND IT      Look the answers up in commentaries if you need.

Why are Cain, Balaam, and Core mentioned here?

_____

_____

_____

_____

_____

Compare these verses in Jude to 2 Peter 2:12-16.  Peter also talks of people who are "spots".  What comparisons can we find between these two passages?

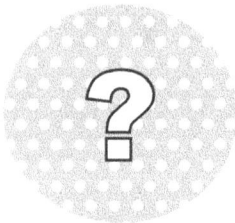

_____

_____

_____

_____

_____

What lessons can you apply from these verses?

_____

_____

_____

_____

_____

_____

# Notes

# Jude vs. 14-16

> 14 And Enoch also, the seventh from Adam, prophesied of these, saying, Behold, the Lord cometh with ten thousands of his saints,
>
> 15 To execute judgment upon all, and to convince all that are ungodly among them of all their ungodly deeds which they have ungodly committed, and of all their hard speeches which ungodly sinners have spoken against him.
>
> 16 These are murmurers, complainers, walking after their own lusts; and their mouth speaketh great swelling words, having men's persons in admiration because of advantage. KJV

Not much is known about Jude's personal life, other than that he was a brother of Jesus.  We don't know how he died, whether by martyrdom or a natural death.  However, we have one of the most pithy, direct books in the Bible that came through this man, Jude.  He wasn't a pushover and he was willing to share his concerns with anyone who would listen.  Jude was a man of great courage.

## DEFINE It

Look up the Greek definitions of these words in the Strong's concordance.

Prophesied: _____

Execute: _____

Hard: _____

Murmurers: _____

Complainers: _____

**My heart**

Am I willing to stand up for truth?  This is a good question, but there is something that comes before standing.  We must first <u>want</u> to know the truth.  Secondly, we must <u>search</u> for it.  Lastly, we must <u>love</u> the truth! Then the standing will come naturally.

Jude 1:14-16

*Lord, I want*

*to understand*

# UNDERSTAND IT

Search the commentaries for an explanation of these phrases found in your verses.  Then write down the explanations to help you better comprehend it.

"execute judgment": _____

_____

_____

"hard speeches": _____

_____

_____

"walking after their own lusts": _____

_____

_____

"great swelling words": _____

_____

_____


# COMPARE IT

Look up these cross references.  They may help you understand your verses in Jude.

Matthew 25:31          Genesis 5:18-24          Deuteronomy 33:2

I Chronicles 1:1-3          Zechariah 14:5

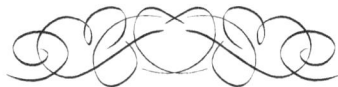


### Just where did Jude get his "extra" information?

Jude must have been an avid reader.  He most likely was quoting from Enoch, a book of the Apocrypha, in verse 14; and from a book called The Assumption of Moses, in verse 9.  These books were not considered inspired by God and therefore, not included in the Bible - but they can sometimes help in understanding culture and history.

"Sanctify them through Thy truth: Thy word is truth."   John 17:17

Jude 1:14-16

COMPREHEND IT        Look the answers up in commentaries if you need.

What are the hard speeches referring to in verse 15?

_____

_____

_____

_____

What does it mean to have men's persons in admiration because of advantage?  And do we ever do this?

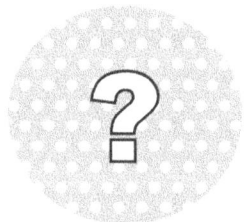

_____

_____

_____

_____

What is something new you learned in these verses?

_____

_____

_____

_____

# Notes

_____

_____

_____

_____

_____

_____

_____

_____

_____

_____

_____

_____

_____

_____

_____

_____

_____

_____

_____

_____

_____

_____

_____

_____

_____

# Jude vs. 17-19

<sup>17</sup> But, beloved, remember ye the words which were spoken before of the apostles of our Lord Jesus Christ;

<sup>18</sup> How that they told you there should be mockers in the last time, who should walk after their own ungodly lusts.

<sup>19</sup> These be they who separate themselves, sensual, having not the Spirit.   KJV

## WORD SEARCH        "false prophet"        "false teacher"

There are many references to false prophets and false teachers within the Bible. Using your search option on eSword, MySword, concordance, or topical dictionary - look up these two words and answer the questions below.

How many times do these terms appear in the Bible? _____

_____

List some of the references you found: _____

_____

_____

Does the Bible ever mention these false prophets and teachers by name? If so, write them down, along with their reference. _____

_____

_____

Was there a common thread you found in the verses you found? _____

_____

_____

What are some of the recurring characteristics of false prophets and teachers that you discovered? _____

_____

_____

## DEFINE IT

Look up the Greek definitions of these words in the Strong's concordance.

Mockers: _____

Separate: _____

Sensual: _____

*Lord, I want to understand*

## UNDERSTAND IT

Search the commentaries for an explanation of these phrases found in your verses.  Then write down the explanations to help you better comprehend it.

"mockers in the last time": _____

_____

_____

"walk after their own ungodly lusts": _____

_____

_____

"separate themselves": _____

_____

_____

"having not the Spirit": _____

_____

_____

## COMPARE IT

Look up these cross references.  They may help you understand your verses in Jude.

Acts 20:29                I Timothy 4:1-2                2 Timothy 3:1-5

2 Peter 2:1-3             2 John 1:7

"Sanctify them through Thy truth: Thy word is truth."   John 17:17

Jude 1:17-19

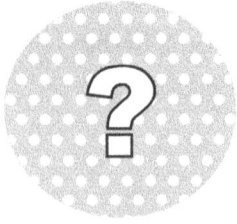

COMPREHEND IT    Look the answers up in commentaries if you need.

What do the lives look like of people who walk after their own ungodly lusts?

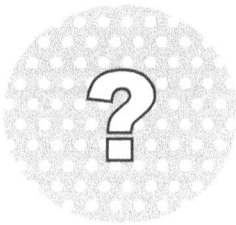

_____

_____

_____

_____

As Christians, how do we walk in the opposite way of those mentioned above?  How do we walk according to the Spirit?

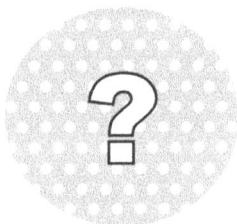

_____

_____

_____

_____

How did God speak to your heart in this lesson?

_____

_____

_____

_____

# Notes

# Jude vs. 20-23

---

<sup>20</sup> But ye, beloved, building up yourselves on your most holy faith, praying in the Holy Ghost,

<sup>21</sup> Keep yourselves in the love of God, looking for the mercy of our Lord Jesus Christ unto eternal life.

<sup>22</sup> And of some have compassion, making a difference:

<sup>23</sup> And others save with fear, pulling them out of the fire; hating even the garment spotted by the flesh. KJV

---

## DEFINE IT

Look up the Greek definitions of these words in the Strong's concordance.

Building: _____

Mercy: _____

Compassion: _____

Hating: _____

Spotted: _____

Flesh: _____

My heart     There comes a time when we must realize how much this faith means to us.  Are we willing to search it out for ourselves . . . love it as our own . . . and stand for it whatever the cost?

"And He said to them all, If any man will come after Me, let him deny himself, and take up his cross daily, and follow Me."  Luke 9:23

"Sanctify them through Thy truth: Thy word is truth."   John 17:17

Jude 1:20-23

*Lord, I want*

*to understand*

# UNDERSTAND IT

Search the commentaries for an explanation of these phrases found in your verses.  Then write down the explanations to help you better comprehend it.

"building up yourselves on your most holy faith": _____

_____

_____

"praying in the Holy Ghost": _____

_____

_____

"of some have compassion": _____

_____

_____

"others save with fear": _____

_____

_____

# COMPARE IT

Look up these cross references.  They may help you understand your verses in Jude.

2 Timothy 1:18            Titus 2:13            Hebrews 9:28

Revelation 3:4            Zechariah 3:2-5       Amos 4:11

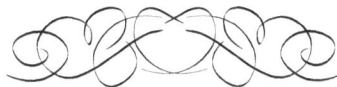

When building up ourselves on the faith, a secure foundation is absolutely necessary. We must have a solid grasp and clear understanding of the Word of God before we can combat the false teachings in the church.

Knowledge of the Word begins with this:  a desire to know and a willingness to learn.

"Sanctify them through Thy truth: Thy word is truth."   John 17:17

Jude 1:20-23

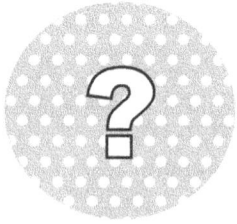

## COMPREHEND IT

How can we pray in the Holy Ghost?  What does this look like in our lives?

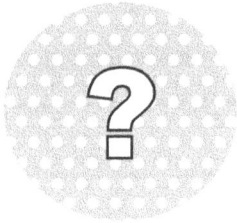

_____

_____

_____

_____

_____

Compare the two ways to help save people:  with compassion and with fear.  Commentaries might help you understand this.

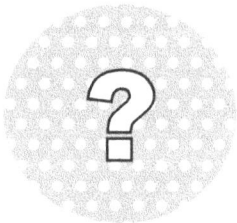

_____

_____

_____

_____

_____

What does it mean to hate the garment spotted by the flesh?

_____

_____

_____

_____

_____

# Notes

_____
_____
_____
_____
_____
_____
_____
_____
_____
_____
_____
_____
_____
_____
_____
_____
_____
_____
_____
_____
_____
_____
_____
_____
_____
_____
_____

# Jude vs. 24-25

<sup>24</sup> Now unto Him that is able to keep you from falling, and to present you faultless before the presence of His glory with exceeding joy,

<sup>25</sup> To the only wise God our Saviour, be glory and majesty, dominion and power, both now and forever.  Amen.   KJV

For the first 80 years of the Christian faith, it was a time of great growth amongst great trials and persecution.  All the writings for the New Testament were completed by AD 80.  By then, the foundation had been laid to spread the Gospel far and wide upon the earth!

Yet Satan had tried his best to infiltrate the Bible with false teaching by sending false teachers amongst the true believers.  This is one of the reasons that makes the book of Jude so valuable.  It was needful for both his time and ours.  Jude stood strong on the truth of God's Word.   May studying this book inspire us to do the same.

## DEFINE IT

Look up the Greek definitions of these words in the Strong's concordance.

Falling: _____

Present: _____

Faultless: _____

Exceeding: _____

Joy: _____

My heart

As we study God's Word, we need to have a heart that is open to both understanding and conviction.  The Holy Spirit can take the words God has inspired and use them to enhance our knowledge of Him . . . while also exposing sin in our hearts.  The deciding factor will be in how we receive it.

"Sanctify them through Thy truth: Thy word is truth."   John 17:17

Jude 1:24-25

*Lord, I want*

*to understand*

# UNDERSTAND IT

Search the commentaries for an explanation of these phrases found in your verses.  Then write down the explanations to help you better comprehend it.

"keep you from falling": _____
_____
_____

"present you faultless": _____
_____
_____

"presence of His glory": _____
_____
_____

"dominion and power": _____
_____
_____

# COMPARE IT

Look up these cross references.  They may help you understand your verses in Jude.

Romans 16:25                2 Corinthians 4:14                Philippians 1:10

I Thessalonians 5:23

Our faith will become sight when we are held up to God the Father - by Jesus our Savior - completely without spot or blemish and shining in His presence.

Oh how wonderful it is that our Savior will do all this - with exultation and welcome!

"Sanctify them through Thy truth: Thy word is truth."   John 17:17

Jude 1:24-25

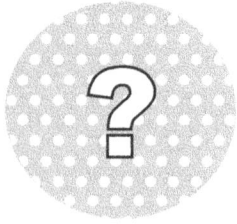

## COMPREHEND IT

How does Jesus keep us from falling?

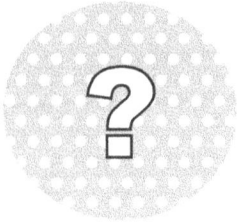

_____

_____

_____

_____

_____

With all the definitions and in-depth study you have just put into verse 24, what does it now mean to you?

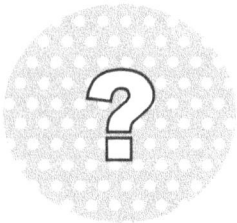

_____

_____

_____

_____

_____

Write two things you have learned from these verses.

_____

_____

_____

_____

_____

# Notes

# From the editors

We hope this study guide has aided in your search for the truth of God's Word.  It is our desire to love the Father and His truth. Even if it means our own hearts must bow in submission to the truths He has revealed to us.

We pray He blesses you in your continued study of the Bible, and as you serve Him.

"Jesus saith unto him, I am the way, the truth, and the life.  No man cometh unto the Father, but by me." John 14:6

He is the only way and He holds all truth.  May He guide you in your study of it . . . and in your search for Him.

www.ingramcontent.com/pod-product-compliance
Lightning Source LLC
Chambersburg PA
CBHW080947050426
42337CB00055B/4726